Classic Poetry for Your Little Genius

Read aloud poems and activities

to enhance early learning

Lilac Mohr

Copyright © 2014 by Lilac Mohr
Illustrations Copyright © Depositphotos.com
All poems and author portraits are in the public domain.
All rights reserved.
ISBN: 1503075214
ISBN-13: 978-1503075214

TABLE OF CONTENTS

Introduction	4
How to Use This Book	5
Emily Dickinson	6
Robert Louis Stevenson	12
Lewis Carroll	18
Edna St. Vincent Millay	24
Robert Frost	30
Christina Rossetti	36
Rudyard Kipling	42
William Wordsworth	48
Edward Lear	54
William Blake	60
Alfred Lord Tennyson	66
William Butler Yeats	72
William Shakespeare	78
Sara Teasdale	84
Henry Wadsworth Longfellow	90
Extra Credit: More Poems to Learn By Heart	96

INTRODUCTION

"What kind of poems should be selected for our children? They must grow up upon the best... There is never a time when they are unequal to worthy thoughts, well put; inspiring tales, well told."
— *Charlotte Mason*

How many five-year-old children do you know who can recite poetry? Of those Kindergarteners, how many have ever heard of Emily Dickinson, Lewis Carroll, Robert Frost, Alfred Lord Tennyson, or William Shakespeare? How many of their parents themselves read poetry on a regular basis? In the modern world, poetry and literature as family entertainment have been replaced by television, video games, computers, and watered-down mass-market books. We are raising a generation of children who are more comfortable with text messaging abbreviations than with using complete sentences and eloquent vocabulary.

When you expose children to poetry from birth, you are giving them a priceless gift. Poetry not only teaches children the mechanics, rhythm, and flow of English, but also how to describe their world and express themselves using beautiful language. Poems can teach children to become better observers, encourage them to explore the natural world, and discover empathy for others. After immersing yourself and your family in poetry, you'll find that your daily life becomes intertwined with the poems that you read: Every animal, plant, and star in the sky will secretly sing to you. If you are skeptical that 18th and 19th century poetry can really change how you see the world, read Blake's "The Tyger" before a trip to the zoo, or Wordsorth's "Daffodils" before going to the botanic gardens, or Dickinson's "The Bee is not Afraid of Me" before a nature walk.

This interactive poetry book contains a selection of classic poems from famous English-language poets to share with your family. Instead of focusing on comprehension and analysis of the poems, which is better suited for older children, each poem is paired with enrichment activities in the areas of visual perception, mathematical reasoning, natural science, and language development. The activities turn the passive act of listening into an engaging experience that allows children to use different areas of their brains.

HOW TO USE THIS BOOK

This book can be used with children from birth to early elementary and beyond. It is best used if you incorporate it into your daily routine. You may choose to read one poem a day, study a different poet each day, or read the book as a bedtime story. The book is meant to be frequently repeated throughout early childhood.

<u>Infants</u>

Read the poems to your baby on a regular basis. Babies will enjoy hearing your voice and the rhythm of the poem. Even newborns will be able to see the high contrast images.

<u>Toddlers</u>

As you read the poems, your toddler will begin to appreciate the structure of the language and rhyming. Point to the images as you name them and count them. Invite your child to point to an image you describe and to count along with you.

<u>Preschoolers</u>

As you read the poems, pause to allow your child to complete the rhyming words. Some preschoolers will be able to complete entire lines from the poem. During each reading, pick one or two of the questions or activities under the picture to complete with your child. For the questions that require using descriptive words, ask prompting questions such as "What do you see/feel/smell?"

<u>Early Elementary</u>

Begin to read the short biographies of each poet and complete the corresponding enrichment activities. After each poem ask your child to explain in his or her words what the poem was about. Identify vocabulary words in each poem and define them for your child. As you read the poems, pause to allow your child to complete entire sections of the poetry. Your child should now be able to complete the additional questions and activities with confidence including descriptive narrations.

EMILY DICKINSON (1830-1886)

Emily Dickinson was an American poet who wrote more than 1,700 poems. She began gardening as a child and kept a book with pressed plants that she labeled. It's not surprising that many of her poems are about nature. When Emily Dickinson was older, she hardly left her house and garden, but wrote many letters to her friends.

<u>Enrichment Activities</u>

- Collect some flowers and leaves and press them between two sheets of paper under a heavy book.

- Write a letter to a friend. Include a poem about nature.

I'M NOBODY! WHO ARE YOU?

Emily Dickinson

I'm Nobody! Who are you?
Are you – Nobody – too?
Then there's a pair of us!
Don't tell! they'd advertise – you know!

How dreary – to be – Somebody!
How public – like a Frog –
To tell one's name – the livelong June –
To an admiring Bog!

Enrichment Questions

- Where does a frog live?

- What does a frog's skin feel like?

- What is special about a frog's legs?

- What are baby frogs called?

THE BEE IS NOT AFRAID OF ME

Emily Dickinson

The Bee is not afraid of me.
I know the Butterfly.
The pretty people in the Woods
Receive me cordially-

The Brooks laugh louder when I come-
The Breezes madder play;
Wherefore mine eye thy silver mists,
Wherefore, Oh Summer's Day?

Enrichment Activity

Find all the pairs of matching butterflies.

"HOPE" IS THE THING WITH FEATHERS

Emily Dickinson

"Hope" is the thing with feathers-
That perches in the soul-
And sings the tune without the words-
And never stops - at all-

And sweetest - in the Gale - is heard-
And sore must be the storm-
That could abash the little Bird
That kept so many warm-

I've heard it in the chillest land-
And on the strangest Sea-
Yet, never, in Extremity,
It asked a crumb - of Me.

<u>Enrichment Questions & Activities</u>

- How many feathers are there?

- Which feather is the longest? Which is the shortest?

- Are feathers light or heavy?

- How many words can you find to describe how a feather feels?

ROBERT LOUIS STEVENSON (1850–1894)

Robert Louis Stevenson was a Scottish author who wrote novels and short stories as well as poems. When he was a child, Robert Louis Stevenson was often sick in bed. He spent this time reading and writing stories. As a young man, Stevenson enjoyed traveling. He had many adventures hiking and canoeing in Europe, crossing the ocean in a steamboat, and traveling across the United States by train.

Enrichment Activities

Tell a story about a trip that you've recently taken. What transportation did you take to get there?

HAPPY THOUGHT

Robert Louis Stevenson

The world is so full of a number of things,
I'm sure we should all be as happy as kings.

Enrichment Questions & Activities

- What are some things that make you happy?

- Describe how a king's life is different from yours.

- Make up a story about the king in the picture.

WHERE GO THE BOATS?

Robert Louis Stevenson

Dark brown is the river,
Golden is the sand.
It flows along for ever,
With trees on either hand.

Green leaves a-floating,
Castles of the foam,
Boats of mine a-boating -
Where will all come home?

On goes the river
And out past the mill,
Away down the valley,
Away down the hill.

Away down the river,
A hundred miles or more,
Other little children
Shall bring my boats ashore.

     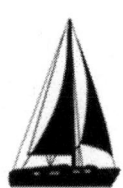

Enrichment Activity

Help the boy find his way through the maze to his boat.

LET BEAUTY AWAKE IN THE MORN...

Robert Louis Stevenson

Let Beauty awake in the morn from beautiful dreams,
Beauty awake from rest!
Let Beauty awake
For Beauty's sake
In the hour when the birds awake in the brake
And the stars are bright in the west!

Let Beauty awake in the eve from the slumber of day,
Awake in the crimson eve!
In the day's dusk end
When the shades ascend,
Let her wake to the kiss of a tender friend
To render again and receive!

Enrichment Questions & Activities

- Find the following: balloon, sandal, pinwheel, ball, truck

- How many children are there in the picture? How many adults?

- Are there more children on the table or on the floor?.

- Which child is youngest?

LEWIS CARROLL (1832-1898)

Lewis Carroll, whose real name was Charles Dodgson, was an English author, mathematician, photographer, and inventor. He is best known for writing nonsense poems, sometimes with words that he made up himself. Many of his poems and stories also contain riddles and logic puzzles.

Enrichment Activities

- What do you think a nonsense poem is like? Come up with some of your own nonsensical sentences.

- Lewis Carroll included many acrostic poems in his works. The first letter of each line of the poem spelled someone's name. Can you come up with a word or sentence for each letter of your name?

from YOU ARE OLD, FATHER WILLIAM
Lewis Carroll

"You are old, Father William," the young man said,
"And your hair has become very white;
And yet you incessantly stand on your head–
Do you think, at your age, it is right?"

Enrichment Questions & Activities

- Place your head and both hands on a mat or carpet to form the three corners of a triangle. Have a grown up help you lift your legs up to perform a headstand. (Warning: supervision required, do not attempt with infants.)

- How old do you think Father William is? What clue is in the poem?

JABBERWOCKY
Lewis Carroll

'Twas brillig, and the slithy toves
Did gyre and gimble in the wabe:
All mimsy were the borogoves,
And the mome raths outgrabe.

"Beware the Jabberwock, my son!
The jaws that bite, the claws that catch!
Beware the Jubjub bird, and shun
The frumious Bandersnatch!"

He took his vorpal sword in hand;
Long time the manxome foe he sought–
So rested he by the Tumtum tree
And stood awhile in thought.

And, as in uffish thought he stood,
The Jabberwock, with eyes of flame,
Came whiffling through the tulgey wood,
And burbled as it came!

One, two! One, two! And through and through
The vorpal blade went snicker-snack!
He left it dead, and with its head
He went galumphing back.

"And hast thou slain the Jabberwock?
Come to my arms, my beamish boy!
O frabjous day! Callooh! Callay!"
He chortled in his joy.

'Twas brillig, and the slithy toves
Did gyre and gimble in the wabe:
All mimsy were the borogoves,
And the mome raths outgrabe.

Enrichment Questions & Activities

- Make up your own word (hint: if you get stuck, try combining two words to form a new one). Put your new word into a sentence.

- Describe the Jabberwocky in your own words.

THE MOCK TURTLE'S SONG

Lewis Carroll

"Will you walk a little faster?" said a whiting to a snail,
"There's a porpoise close behind us, and he's treading on my tail.
See how eagerly the lobsters and the turtles all advance!
They are waiting on the shingle – will you come and join the dance?
Will you, won't you, will you, won't you, will you join the dance?
Will you, won't you, will you, won't you, won't you join the dance?

"You can really have no notion how delightful it will be
When they take us up and throw us, with the lobsters, out to sea!"
But the snail replied "Too far, too far!" and gave a look askance –
Said he thanked the whiting kindly, but he would not join the dance.
Would not, could not, would not, could not, would not join the dance.
Would not, could not, would not, could not, could not join the dance.

"What matters it how far we go?" his scaly friend replied,
"There is another shore, you know, upon the other side.
The further off from England the nearer is to France –
Then turn not pale, beloved snail, but come and join the dance.
Will you, won't you, will you, won't you, will you join the dance?
Will you, won't you, will you, won't you, won't you join the dance?"

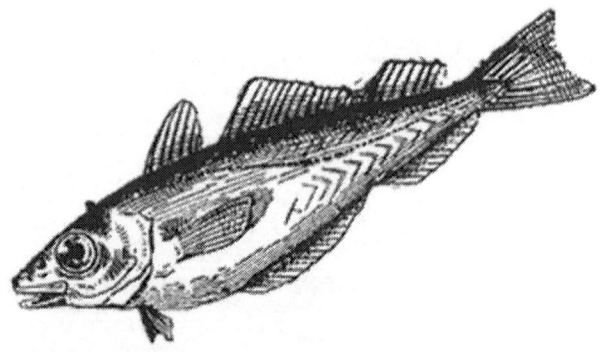

Enrichment Activity

Find the following:
- one octopus
- two sea horses
- two lobsters
- three dolphins
- seven sea stars

EDNA ST. VINCENT MILLAY (1892-1950)

Edna St. Vincent Millay was an American poet and playwright who was awarded the Pulitzer Prize for her poetry. When she was a child, Millay and her two sisters had to do chores around the house while her mother worked as a nurse. They made the household tasks into games. Her mother did not have much money, but encouraged her daughters to read books, play the piano, and learn different languages.

<u>Enrichment Questions & Activities</u>

- Make a list of tasks that you have to do around the house. How can you make those tasks into games?

- Edna St. Vincent Millay spoke six languages. Can you say "Hello" in another language?

FIRST FIG

Edna St. Vincent Millay

My candle burns at both ends;
It will not last the night;
But ah, my foes, and oh, my friends—
It gives a lovely light!

Enrichment Questions

- Which candle is tallest? Which is shortest?

- Which candle is thickest? Which is thinnest?

- Are there more candles which are lit or burned out?

CITY TREES

Edna St. Vincent Millay

The trees along this city street,
Save for the traffic and the trains,
Would make a sound as thin and sweet
As trees in country lanes.

And people standing in their shade
Out of a shower, undoubtedly
Would hear such music as is made
Upon a country tree.

Oh, little leaves that are so dumb
Against the shrieking city air,
I watch you when the wind has come–
I know what sound is there.

Enrichment Questions and Activities

- Touch the trees in order from one to twelve.

- Can you find more trees in the city or the country? Why is it harder to hear the city trees?

- What do trees sound like? Make up a song of the trees.

AFTERNOON ON A HILL

Edna St. Vincent Millay

I will be the gladdest thing
Under the sun!
I will touch a hundred flowers
And not pick one.

I will look at cliffs and clouds
With quiet eyes,
Watch the wind bow down the grass,
And the grass rise.

And when lights begin to show
Up from the town,
I will mark which must be mine,
And then start down!

Enrichment Activities

- Match each flower to its silhouette.

- Pretend you are in a wildflower meadow. Paint a picture with your words. Describe what you see, hear, smell, and feel.

ROBERT FROST (1874-1963)

Robert Frost was an American poet who won the Pulitzer Prize four times. Although he grew up in the city, Frost longed to live in the country. As an adult, he bought a farm in New Hampshire. Robert Frost would write poems early in the morning, and then work on the farm the rest of the day. He is best known for his poems about rural life.

Enrichment Questions

- What is the difference between rural living and urban living? Do you live in an urban, suburban, or rural location?

- What are some jobs you would have if you lived on a farm?

PUTTING IN THE SEED

Robert Frost

You come to fetch me from my work to-night
When supper's on the table, and we'll see
If I can leave off burying the white
Soft petals fallen from the apple tree
(Soft petals, yes, but not so barren quite,
Mingled with these, smooth bean and wrinkled pea);
And go along with you ere you lose sight
Of what you came for and become like me,
Slave to a Springtime passion for the earth.
How Love burns through the Putting in the Seed
On through the watching for that early birth
When, just as the soil tarnishes with weed,
The sturdy seedling with arched body comes
Shouldering its way and shedding the earth crumbs.

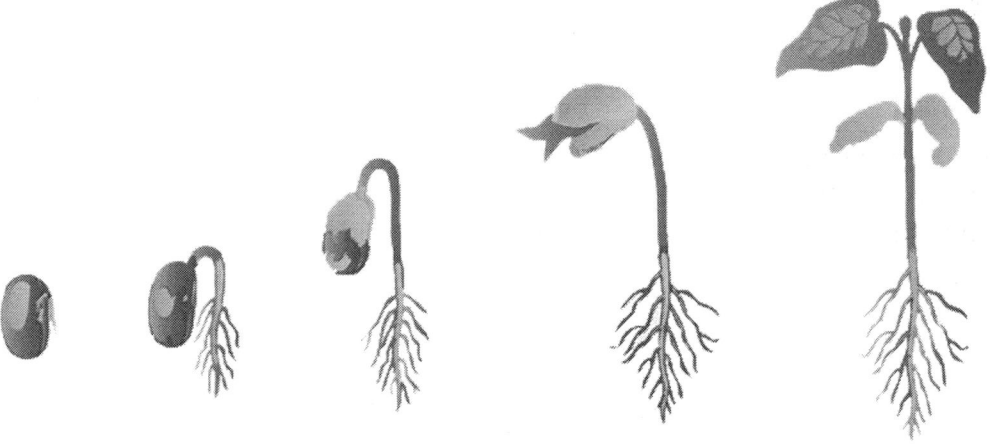

Enrichment Activity

Describe how a seed grows into a plant. What happens first, second, third, and fourth? What do you think will happen next?

THE ROAD NOT TAKEN
Robert Frost

Two roads diverged in a yellow wood,
And sorry I could not travel both
And be one traveler, long I stood
And looked down one as far as I could
To where it bent in the undergrowth;

Then took the other, as just as fair,
And having perhaps the better claim
Because it was grassy and wanted wear,
Though as for that the passing there
Had worn them really about the same,

And both that morning equally lay
In leaves no step had trodden black.
Oh, I kept the first for another day!
Yet knowing how way leads on to way
I doubted if I should ever come back.

I shall be telling this with a sigh
Somewhere ages and ages hence:
Two roads diverged in a wood, and I,
I took the one less traveled by,
And that has made all the difference.

Enrichment Questions and Activity

• Use your finger to find a path through the maze

• Describe a time that you had to make a decision. How did you decide which option to select?

THE PASTURE
Robert Frost

I'm going out to clean the pasture spring;
I'll only stop to rake the leaves away
(And wait to watch the water clear, I may):
I shan't be gone long.–You come too.

I'm going out to fetch the little calf
That's standing by the mother. It's so young,
It totters when she licks it with her tongue.
I shan't be gone long.–You come too.

Enrichment Activity

Find the following:

- A calf's mother
- A lamb's mother
- A foal's mother
- Three birds
- An animal that says "hee-haw"
- Two animals that people keep in the house as pets

CHRISTINA ROSSETTI (1830-1894)

Christina Rossetti was an English poet. She came from a family of writers and artists. Her brother Dante painted this portrait of her. The children of the family made their own family newspaper which included some of Christina Rossetti's first poems. Her nature poems were inspired by the time she spent at her grandfather's country cottage. She was also devout to her Christian faith. Rossetti became one of the most famous female poets of her time.

Enrichment Activity

Make your own family newspaper.
You can include artwork, stories, and poems.

FLY AWAY, FLY AWAY OVER THE SEA
Christina Rossetti

Fly away, fly away over the sea,
Sun-loving swallow, for summer is done;
Come again, come again, come back to me,
Bringing the summer and bringing the sun.

Enrichment Activity

Find the following summer objects:
- Three things that you wear
- Two toys to take to the beach
- Five seashells
- Four things that protect you from the sun
- Three things that are alive

WHAT DO THE STARS DO?

Christina Rossetti

What do the stars do
Up in the sky,
Higher than the wind can blow,
Or the clouds can fly?
Each star in its own glory
Circles, circles still;
As it was lit to shine and set,
And do its Maker's will.

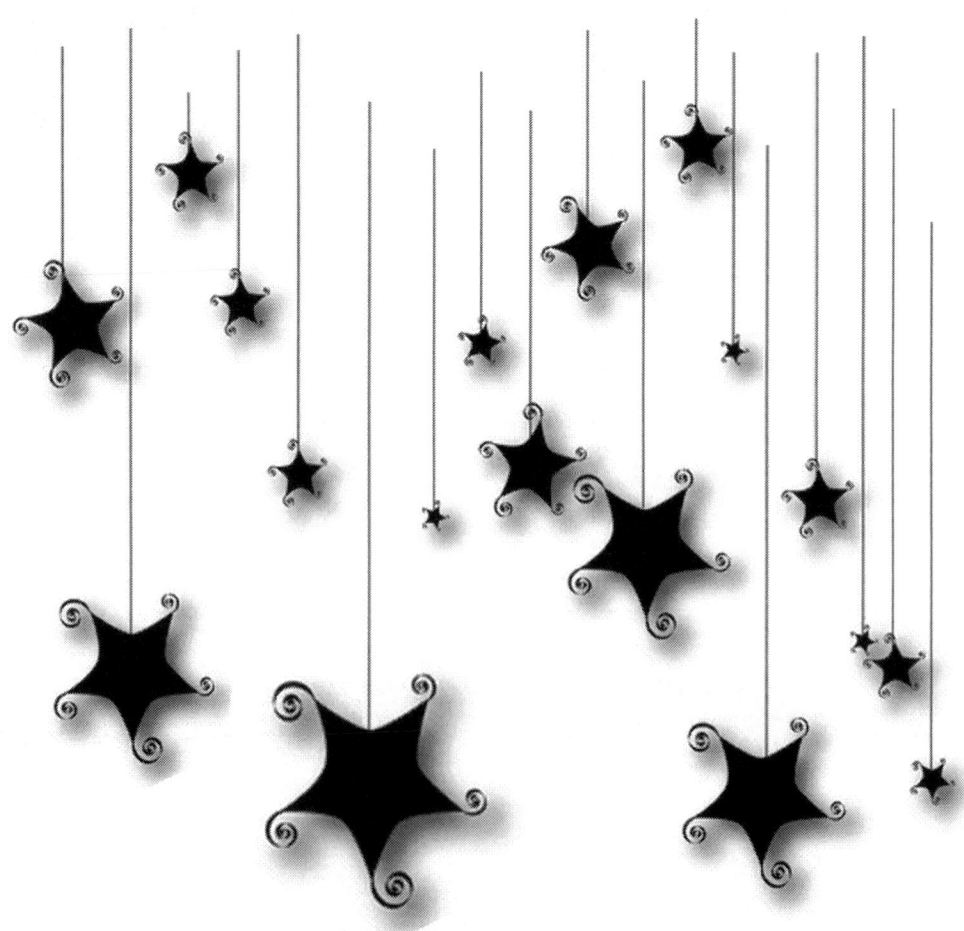

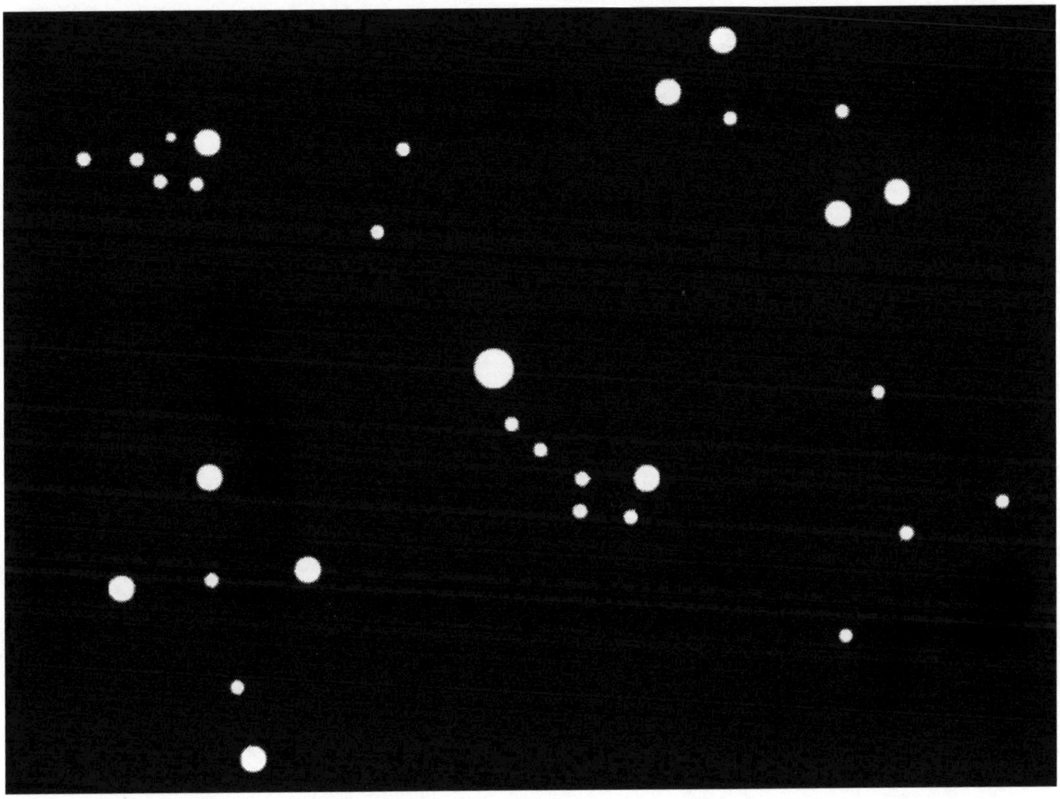

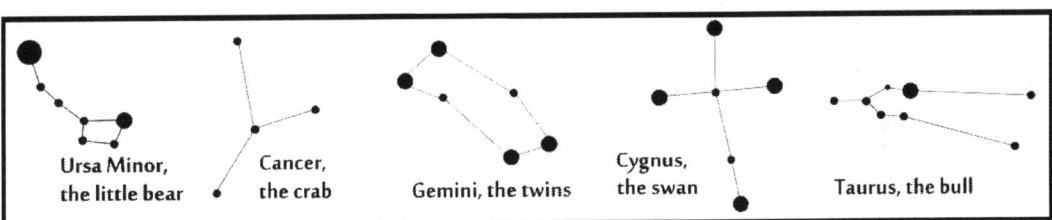

Enrichment Questions & Activities

- Find each constellation in the picture.

- Make up your own constellation by making some dots on a separate piece of paper and connecting them to form the shape of an object.

A BIRTHDAY

Christina Rossetti

My heart is like a singing bird
Whose nest is in a water'd shoot;
My heart is like an apple-tree
Whose boughs are bent with thickset fruit;
My heart is like a rainbow shell
That paddles in a halcyon sea;
My heart is gladder than all these
Because my love is come to me.

Raise me a dais of silk and down;
Hang it with vair and purple dyes;
Carve it in doves and pomegranates,
And peacocks with a hundred eyes;
Work it in gold and silver grapes,
In leaves and silver fleurs-de-lys;
Because the birthday of my life
Is come, my love is come to me.

Enrichment Questions & Activities

- Find each pair of matching hearts.

- Finish this sentence in your own words:
  "My heart is like _____."

RUDYARD KIPLING (1865-1936)

Rudyard Kipling was an English author who wrote poems, short stories, and novels. He was born in India but went to school in England when he was six years old. When he was sixteen, Kipling returned to India which is the setting for his most famous novel, The Jungle Book. During his life, Rudyard Kipling traveled to China, Japan, South Africa, the United States, and Canada. He became the first English author to win the Nobel Prize in Literature.

Enrichment Activities

- Find all the countries that Rudyard Kipling visited on a world map.

- Rudyard Kipling included poems inside many of his short stories and novels. Write a poem, and then turn it into a story.

SEAL LULLABY

Rudyard Kipling

Oh! hush thee, my baby, the night is behind us,
And black are the waters that sparkled so green.
The moon, o'er the combers, looks downward to find us
At rest in the hollows that rustle between.
Where billow meets billow, then soft be thy pillow,
Ah, weary wee flipperling, curl at thy ease!
The storm shall not wake thee, nor shark overtake thee,
Asleep in the arms of the slow-swinging seas!

Enrichment Questions

- What do seals have to make them good swimmers?

- How do seals keep warm in the cold ocean?

- Do seals lay eggs or give birth to their babies?

- What do baby seals drink after they are born?

THE CAMEL'S HUMP

Rudyard Kipling

The Camel's hump is an ugly lump
Which well you may see at the Zoo;
But uglier yet is the hump we get
From having too little to do.

Kiddies and grown-ups too-oo-oo,
If we haven't enough to do-oo-oo,
We get the hump–
Cameelious hump–
The hump that is black and blue!

We climb out of bed with a frouzly head,
And a snarly-yarly voice.
We shiver and scowl and we grunt and we growl
At our bath and our boots and our toys;

And there ought to be a corner for me
(And I know' there is one for you)
When we get the hump–
Cameelious hump–
The hump that is black and blue!

The cure for this ill is not to sit still,
Or frowst with a book by the fire;
But to take a large hoe and a shovel also,
And dig till you gently perspire;

And then you will find that the sun and the wind,
And the Djinn of the Garden too,
Have lifted the hump-
The horrible hump-
The hump that is black and blue!

I get it as well as you-oo-oo-
If I haven't enough to do-oo-oo!
We all get hump-
Cameelious hump-
Kiddies and grown-ups too!

Enrichment Questions & Activities

- Which camel is first? Which is last?

- How many people does the third camel have on its back?

- Without counting, figure out if there are more camels or people in the picture. How do you know? Count to check your answer.

- What are some things you do when you are bored or grumpy?

HUNTING SONG OF THE SEEONEE PACK
Rudyard Kipling

As the dawn was breaking the Sambhur belled
Once, twice, and again!

And a doe leaped up -
   and a doe leaped up
From the pond in the wood
     where the wild deer sup.
This I, scouting alone, beheld,
Once, twice, and again!

As the dawn was breaking the Sambhur belled
Once, twice, and again!

And a wolf stole back – and a wolf stole back
To carry the word to the waiting Pack;
And we sought and we found and we bayed on his track
Once, twice, and again!

As the dawn was breaking the Wolf-pack yelled
Once, twice, and again!

Feet in the jungle that leave no mark!
Eyes that can see in the dark – the dark!
Tongue – give tongue to it! Hark! O Hark!
Once, twice, and again!

Enrichment Questions & Activities

- Match each animal to its tracks.

- Which of the animals are predators and which are prey?

- Clap your hands "once, twice, and again." How many times did you clap?

WILLIAM WORDSWORTH (1770-1850)

William Wordsworth was an English poet who set out to create a new type of poetry for his day. The Romantic poetry that he wrote was about human emotions. He used ordinary language that average people could understand.

Enrichment Activities

- Make a list of emotions (such as happy, sad, excited, surprised, etc..)

- Pick one of those emotions and write a poem that makes the reader feel that emotion.

UPON WESTMINSTER BRIDGE

William Wordsworth

Earth has not anything to show more fair:
Dull would he be of soul who could pass by
A sight so touching in its majesty:
This City now doth like a garment wear

The beauty of the morning: silent, bare,
Ships, towers, domes, theatres, and temples lie
Open unto the fields, and to the sky,
All bright and glittering in the smokeless air.

Never did sun more beautifully steep
In his first splendour valley, rock, or hill;
Ne'er saw I, never felt, a calm so deep!

The river glideth at his own sweet will:
Dear God! the very houses seem asleep;
And all that mighty heart is lying still!

Enrichment Question

Can you find Big Ben the clock tower in this picture of the Westminster Bridge in London?

DAFFODILS

William Wordsworth

I wandered lonely as a cloud
That floats on high o'er vales and hills,
When all at once I saw a crowd,
A host, of golden daffodils;
Beside the lake, beneath the trees,
Fluttering and dancing in the breeze.

Continuous as the stars that shine
And twinkle on the milky way,
They stretched in never-ending line
Along the margin of a bay:
Ten thousand saw I at a glance,
Tossing their heads in sprightly dance.

The waves beside them danced; but they
Out-did the sparkling waves in glee:
A poet could not but be gay,
In such a jocund company:
I gazed-and gazed-but little thought
What wealth the show to me had brought:

For oft, when on my couch I lie
In vacant or in pensive mood,
They flash upon that inward eye
Which is the bliss of solitude;
And then my heart with pleasure fills,
And dances with the daffodils.

Enrichment Questions & Activities

- Estimate the number of daffodils in the picture. Is it less than 100 or more than 100? Is it less than 5 or more than 5?

- Count the daffodils to check your estimate. Try counting by fives.

from THE KITTEN AND FALLING LEAVES
William Wordsworth

See the kitten on the wall, sporting with the leaves that fall,
Withered leaves-one-two-and three, from the lofty elder-tree!
Through the calm and frosty air, of this morning bright and fair ...
-But the kitten, how she starts; Crouches, stretches, paws, and darts!

First at one, and then its fellow, just as light and just as yellow;
There are many now-now one-now they stop and there are none;
What intenseness of desire, in her upward eye of fire!

With a tiger-leap half way, now she meets the coming prey,
Lets it go as fast, and then, has it in her power again:
Now she works with three or four, like an Indian Conjuror;
Quick as he in feats of art, far beyond in joy of heart.

Enrichment Questions & Activities

- Can you find a rake and a wheelbarrow in the picture? What are they used for?

- What season is shown in the picture? How do you know?

- Count the number of geese flying in the sky. What shape are they flying in?

- Come up with different ways to play with autumn leaves. Pretend you are playing these games using imaginary leaves.

EDWARD LEAR (1812–1888)

Edward Lear was an English poet, artist, and musician. He illustrated many of his own poems and drew his own self-portrait above. Lear played many musical instruments including the piano, accordion, flute, and guitar. He composed music to go with poetry. Edward Lear always felt out of place in the world and often wrote nonsense poems about characters who were different from others but accepted who they were.

Enrichment Activities

- Draw your own self-portrait.

- Pretend to play the various instruments that Edward Lear played using imaginary instruments.

- Pick a poem and write music to go along with it. You can hum the melody or play it on a real instrument.

from HOW PLEASANT TO KNOW MR. LEAR

Edward Lear

How pleasant to know Mr. Lear,
Who has written such volumes of stuff.
Some think him ill-tempered and queer,
But a few find him pleasant enough.

His mind is concrete and fastidious,
His nose is remarkably big;
His visage is more or less hideous,
His beard it resembles a wig.

When he walks in waterproof white,
The children run after him so!
Calling out, "He's gone out in his night-
Gown, that crazy old Englishman, oh!"

He weeps by the side of the ocean,
He weeps on the top of the hill;
He purchases pancakes and lotion,
And chocolate shrimps from the mill.

He reads, but he does not speak, Spanish,
He cannot abide ginger beer;
Ere the days of his pilgrimage vanish,
How pleasant to know Mr. Lear!

Enrichment Activity

Write a poem about how pleasant it is to know *you*.

THE OWL AND THE PUSSYCAT
Edward Lear

The Owl and the Pussy Cat went to sea
In a beautiful pea-green boat,
They took some honey, and plenty of money
Wrapped up in a five-pound note.
The Owl looked up to the stars above,
And sang to a small guitar,
"O lovely Pussy, O Pussy, my love,
What a beautiful Pussy you are,
You are,
You are!
What a beautiful Pussy you are!"

Pussy said to the Owl, "You elegant fowl!
How charmingly sweet you sing!
O let us be married! too long we have tarried:
But what shall we do for a ring?"
They sailed away, for a year and a day,
To the land where the Bong-tree grows
And there in a wood a Piggy-wig stood
With a ring at the end of his nose,
His nose,
His nose,
With a ring at the end of his nose.

"Dear Pig, are you willing to sell for one shilling
Your ring?" Said the Piggy, "I will."
So they took it away, and were married next day
By the Turkey who lives on the hill.
They dined on mince, and slices of quince,
Which they ate with a runcible spoon;
And hand in hand, on the edge of the sand,
They danced by the light of the moon,
The moon,
The moon,
They danced by the light of the moon.

Illustrations by William Foster (1889)

Enrichment Activity

- Point to the pictures in the correct order.
- What adventures do you think the Owl and Pussycat will have next?

from THE SCROOBIOUS PIP

Edward Lear

The Scroobious Pip went out one day
When the grass was green, and the sky was grey.
Then all the beasts in the world came round
When the Scroobious Pip sat down on the ground.
The cat and the dog and the kangaroo
The sheep and the cow and the guineapig too-
The wolf he howled, the horse he neighed
The little pig squeaked and the donkey brayed,
And when the lion began to roar
There never was heard such a noise before.
And every beast he stood on the tip
Of his toes to look at the Scroobious Pip.

At last they said to the Fox – "By far,
You're the wisest beast! You know you are!
Go close to Scroobious Pip and say,
Tell us all about yourself we pray-

For as yet we can't make out in the least
If you're Fish or Insect, or Bird or Beast."
The Scroobious Pip looked vaguelyy round
And sang these words with a rumbling sound-
Chippetty Flip; Flippetty Chip;-
My only name is the Scroobious Pip.

Enrichment Questions and Activities

- Find the following creatures:
  - with three eyes
  - with four arms and four legs
  - with a bow
  - with no arms and no legs
  - covered in fur.

- Describe what you think the Scroobious Pip is like. How does he look? How does he behave?

WILLIAM BLAKE (1757-1827)

William Blake was an English painter and poet. From an early age, he claimed to have visions of God and angels. Religion played a large role in Blake's art and poetry. As an artist, he is best known for relief etchings where special tools were used to engrave drawings on pieces of metal (usually copper).

Enrichment Activity

Use a piece of aluminum foil and a dull pencil to carefully create your own etching.

SPRING

William Blake

Sound the flute!
Now it's mute.
Birds delight
Day and night.
Nightingale
In the dale,
Lark in the sky,
Merrily,
Merrily, merrily to welcome in the year.

Little boy
Full of joy,
Little girl
Sweet and small.
Cock does crow,
So do you.
Merry voice,
Infant noise,
Merrily, merrily to welcome in the year.

Little lamb
Here I am
Come and lick
My white neck.
Let me pull
Your soft wool.
Let me kiss
Your soft face,
Merrily, merrily we welcome in the year.

THE NURSE'S SONG (from SONGS OF INNOCENCE)
William Blake

When voices of children are heard on the green
And laughing is heard on the hill,
My heart is at rest within my breast
And everything else is still

Then come home my children the sun is gone down
And the dews of night arise
Come come leave off play, and let us away
Till the morning appears in the skies

No no let us play, for it is yet day
And we cannot go to sleep
Besides in the sky, the little birds fly
And the hills are all covered with sheep

Well well go and play till the light fades away
And then go home to bed
The little ones leaped and shouted and laughed
And all the hills echoed

<u>Enrichment Questions and Activities</u>

- Touch the children in order from one to fourteen
- Are more children facing to the left or to the right?
- Choose a child and describe what he or she is doing.

THE TYGER

William Blake

Tyger Tyger, burning bright,
In the forests of the night;
What immortal hand or eye,
Could frame thy fearful symmetry?

In what distant deeps or skies.
Burnt the fire of thine eyes?
On what wings dare he aspire?
What the hand, dare seize the fire?

And what shoulder, and what art,
Could twist the sinews of thy heart?
And when thy heart began to beat,
What dread hand? and what dread feet?

What the hammer? what the chain,
In what furnace was thy brain?
What the anvil? what dread grasp,
Dare its deadly terrors clasp!

When the stars threw down their spears
And watered heaven with their tears:
Did he smile his work to see?
Did he who made the Lamb make thee?

Tyger Tyger burning bright,
In the forests of the night:
What immortal hand or eye,
Dare frame thy fearful symmetry?

Enrichment Activity

- Find the images that are symmetrical. Use your fingers to show the line of symmetry.

- On a separate piece of paper, make a symmetrical drawing.

ALFRED LORD TENNYSON (1809-1892)

Alfred Lord Tennyson is one of the best known British poets. When he was only 12, he wrote a 6,000 line epic poem. As an adult, Tennyson was appointed Poet Laureate for Great Britain and Ireland. It was his job to write poems for important national events.

Enrichment Activities

- Make a list of different occasions such as birthdays, holidays, weddings, birth of a baby, losing a tooth, etc..

- Pretend that you are Poet Laureate of your household. Choose one occasion from your list and write or draw something special for that event.

THE OWL

Alfred Lord Tennyson

When cats run home and light is come,
And dew is cold upon the ground,
And the far-off stream is dumb,
And the whirring sail goes round,
And the whirring sail goes round;
Alone and warming his five wits,
The white owl in the belfry sits.

When merry milkmaids click the latch,
And rarely smells the new-mown hay,
And the cock hath sung beneath the thatch
Twice or thrice his roundelay,
Twice or thrice his roundelay;
Alone and warming his five wits,
The white owl in the belfry sits.

Enrichment Questions and Activities

- Find all pairs of matching owls.
- Owls are nocturnal. What other animals are nocturnal?

from SEA DREAMS {CRADLE SONG}
Alfred Lord Tennyson

What does little birdie say
In her nest at peep of day?
Let me fly, says little birdie,
Mother, let me fly away.
Birdie, rest a little longer,
Till thy little wings are stronger.
So she rests a little longer,
Then she flies away.

What does little baby say,
In her bed at peep of day?
Baby says, like little birdie,
Let me rise and fly away.
Baby, sleep a little longer,
Till thy little limbs are stronger.
If she sleeps a little longer,
Baby too shall fly away.

Enrichment Questions and Activities

- Tell a story about the boy and the bird that you see in the picture.

- How do birds take care of their babies? How do humans take care of their babies?

- Can the human baby really fly away? Compare how different animals move.

- What special features do birds have to give them the ability to fly?

from THE PRINCESS {SWEET AND LOW}
Alfred Lord Tennyson

Sweet and low, sweet and low,
Wind of the western sea,
Low, low, breathe and blow,
Wind of the western sea!
Over the rolling waters go,
Come from the dying moon, and blow,
Blow him again to me;
While my little one,
    while my pretty one, sleeps.

    Sleep and rest, sleep and rest,
    Father will come to thee soon;
    Rest, rest, on mother's breast,
    Father will come to thee soon;
    Father will come to his babe in the nest,
    Silver sails all out of the west
    Under the silver moon:
    Sleep, my little one,
        sleep, my pretty one, sleep.

Enrichment Questions and Activities

- Count the boats in each of these categories: one sail, two sails, three sails, more than three sails, no sails.

- Wind pushes sailboats through the water. What moves boats without sails through the water?

- What is wrong with the proportions in the picture above? How do the sizes of these boats compare in real life?

WILLIAM BUTLER YEATS (1865-1939)

William Butler Yeats was an Irish poet and playwright. He won the Nobel Prize for Literature in 1923. Ever since childhood, he was fascinated by Irish folklore and was a believer in fairies, ghosts, and the supernatural. Yeats later turned many of Ireland's myths and legends into poems.

<u>Enrichment Activity</u>

Pick a fairy tale or legend. Write a poem, draw a picture, or perform a play inspired by the story you chose.

THE LAKE ISLE OF INNISFREE

William Butler Yeats

I will arise and go now, and go to Innisfree,
And a small cabin build there, of clay and wattles made:
Nine bean-rows will I have there, a hive for the honey-bee;
And live alone in the bee-loud glade.

And I shall have some peace there, for peace comes dropping slow,
Dropping from the veils of the morning to where the cricket sings;
There midnight's all a glimmer, and noon a purple glow,
And evening full of the linnet's wings.

I will arise and go now, for always night and day
I hear lake water lapping with low sounds by the shore;
While I stand on the roadway, or on the pavements grey,
I hear it in the deep heart's core.

Enrichment Questions and Activities

- What does a bee-loud glade sound like? What are some other sounds of nature?

- Imagine a beautiful place that you can escape to in your imagination when you feel sad or upset. Draw a picture of this place on a separate piece of paper

THE SONG OF WANDERING AENGUS

William Butler Yeats

I went out to the hazel wood,
Because a fire was in my head,
And cut and peeled a hazel wand,
And hooked a berry to a thread;
And when white moths were on the wing,
And moth-like stars were flickering out,
I dropped the berry in a stream
And caught a little silver trout.

When I had laid it on the floor
I went to blow the fire a-flame,
But something rustled on the floor,
And some one called me by my name:
It had become a glimmering girl
With apple blossom in her hair
Who called me by my name and ran
And faded through the brightening air.

Though I am old with wandering
Through hollow lands and hilly lands,
I will find out where she has gone,
And kiss her lips and take her hands;
And walk among long dappled grass,
And pluck till time and times are done
The silver apples of the moon,
The golden apples of the sun.

Enrichment Activity

Use your finger to find your way through the maze.

75

THE CAT AND THE MOON

William Butler Yeats

The cat went here and there
And the moon spun round like a top,
And the nearest kin of the moon,
The creeping cat, looked up.
Black Minnaloushe stared at the moon,
For, wander and wail as he would,
The pure cold light in the sky
Troubled his animal blood.

Minnaloushe runs in the grass
Lifting his delicate feet.
Do you dance, Minnaloushe, do you dance?
When two close kindred meet,
What better than call a dance?
Maybe the moon may learn,
Tired of that courtly fashion,
A new dance turn.
Minnaloushe creeps through the grass
From moonlit place to place,
The sacred moon overhead
Has taken a new phase.

Does Minnaloushe know that his pupils
Will pass from change to change,
And that from round to crescent,
From crescent to round they range?
Minnaloushe creeps through the grass
Alone, important and wise,
And lifts to the changing moon
His changing eyes.

76

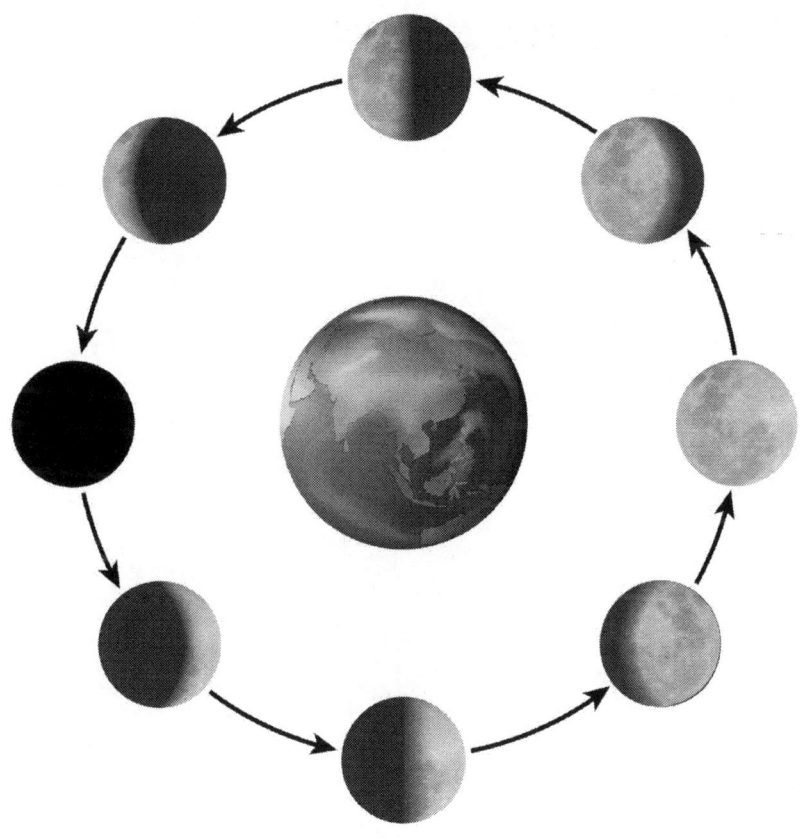

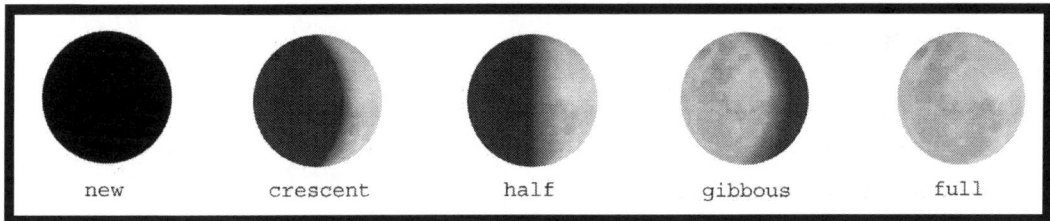

Enrichment Questions & Activities

- Find the moon phases in the picture.

- Does the earth go around the moon or the moon go around the earth?

- Find the images that show the lit part of the moon on the right (called "waxing"). Find the images where the lit part of the moon is on the left (called "waning").

WILLIAM SHAKESPEARE (1564-1616)

William Shakespeare was an English playwright, actor, and poet. He wrote over 150 sonnets (or poems) and over thirty plays which are still performed today. Shakespeare is associated with the Globe Theatre, a three-story circular amphitheater where as many as 3,000 people could watch performances of his plays.

Enrichment Activities

- William Shakespeare wrote plays that fall into three genres: comedy, tragedy, and history. Give an example of events that might happen that would fit in each of these categories.

- Make your own puppets and use them to put on a play for your family and friends.

URCHIN'S DANCE

William Shakespeare

By the moone we sport and play,
With the night begins our day;
As we frisk the dew doth fall, Trip it, little urchins all,
Lightly as the little bee.
Two by two, and three by three.
And about goe wee, goe wee.

<u>Enrichment Activity</u>

Look at each pattern of dancing gnomes to figure out which kind of gnome will come next.

IF YOU SEE A FAERY RING

William Shakespeare

If you see a faery ring
In a field of grass,
Very lightly step around,
Tip-toe as you pass,
Last night faeries frolicked there
And they're sleeping somewhere near.

If you see a tiny faery,
Lying fast asleep
Shut your eyes
And run away,
Do not stay to peek!
Do not tell
Or you'll break a faery spell.

Illustration by Richard Doyle 1870

Illustration by Richard Doyle 1870

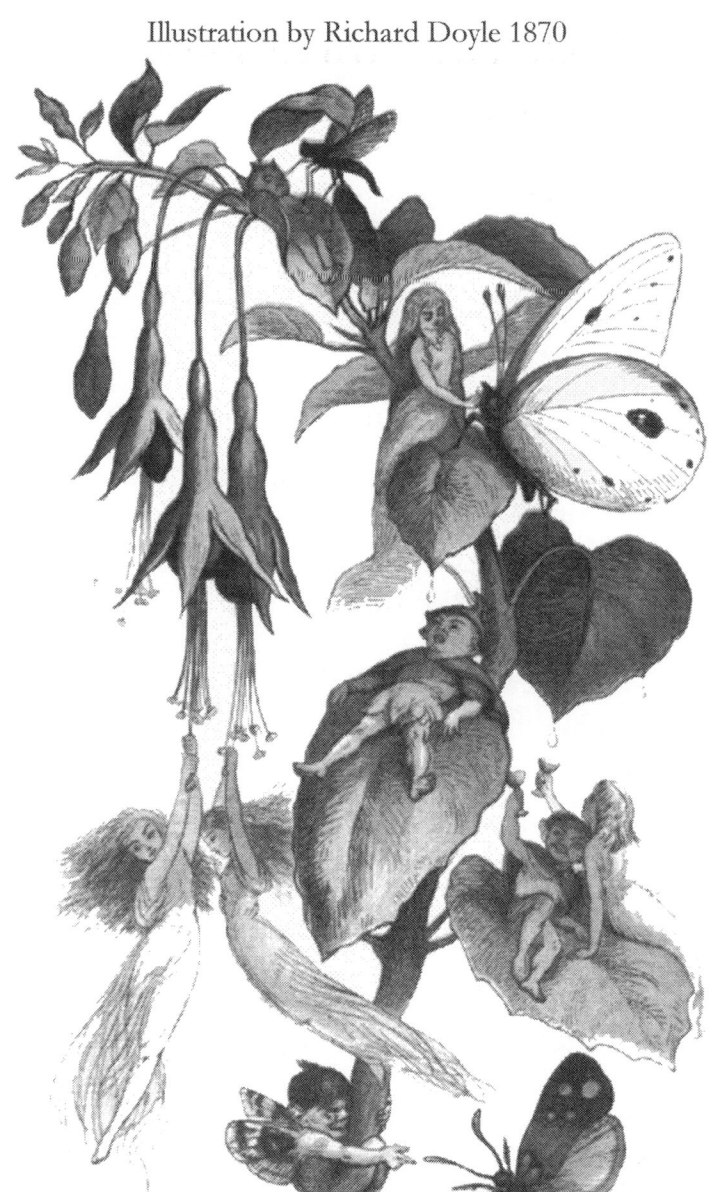

Enrichment Questions & Activities

- Count the number of fairy-folk in the picture.

- Are there more girl fairies or boy fairies?

- Pick a fairy and describe what he or she is doing.

SONG OF THE HOLLY
William Shakespeare

Blow, blow thou winter wind,
Thou art not so unkind
As man's ingratitude!
Thy tooth is not so keen,
Because thou art not seen,
Although thy breath be rude.

Heigh ho! sing heigh ho! unto the green holly,
Most friendship is feigning, most loving mere folly.
Then heigh ho! the holly!
This life is most jolly!

Freeze, freeze, thou bitter sky,
Thou dost not bite so nigh
As benefits forgot!
Though thou the waters warp,
Thy sting is not so sharp
As friend remembered not.

Heigh ho! sing heigh ho! unto the green holly,
Most friendship is feigning, most loving mere folly.
Then heigh ho, the holly!
This life is most jolly!

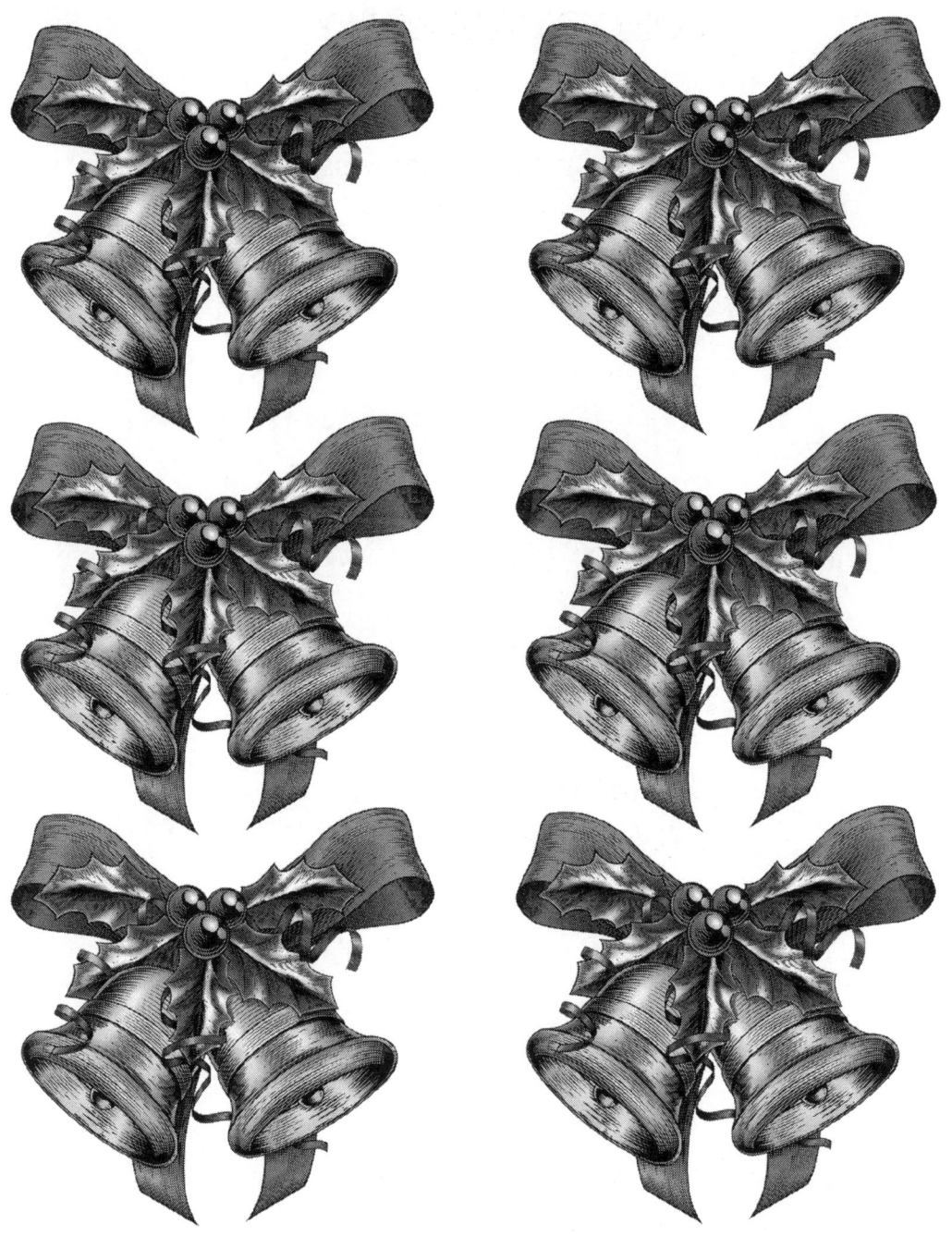

Enrichment Activity

Count the following objects in the holly decorations:
- Bows (count by 1s)
- Bells (skip count by 2s)
- Berries (skip count by 3s)
- Leaves of holly (skip count by 5s)

SARA TEASDALE (1884-1933)

Sara Teasdale was an American poet who was very popular in her day. She earned the first Pulitzer Prize in Poetry. Sara Teasdate was frequently ill as a child and spent most of her childhood at home. Her mother said that her first word was "pretty". Teasdale's love of beauty resonates through her poetry.

Enrichment Activities

- Write a poem about something beautiful.

- On a separate piece of paper make an award and present it to someone who deserves it.

APRIL

Sara Teasdale

The roofs are shining from the rain.
The sparrows tritter as they fly,
And with a windy April grace
The little clouds go by.

Yet the back-yards are bare and brown
With only one unchanging tree-
I could not be so sure of Spring
Save that it sings in me.

Enrichment Questions and Activities

- Define evaporation, condensation, precipitation (rain), and runoff.
- Use the diagram to tell the story of the water cycle.

from A BALLAD OF TWO KNIGHTS

Sara Teasdale

Two knights rode forth at early dawn
A-seeking maids to wed,
Said one, "My lady must be fair,
With gold hair on her head."

Then spake the other knight-at-arms:
"I care not for her face,
But she I love must be a dove
For purity and grace."

And each knight blew upon his horn
And went his separate way,
And each knight found a lady-love
Before the fall of day.

But she was brown who should have had
The shining yellow hair,
I ween the knights forgot their words
Or else they ceased to care.

For he who wanted purity
Brought home a wanton wild,
And when each saw the other knight
I seen that each knight smiled.

Enrichment Questions and Activities

- Find the larger number in each pair of knights to find the winner
- Make a list of characteristics that you look for in a friend.

SNOW SONG
Sara Teasdale

Fairy snow, fairy snow,
Blowing, blowing everywhere,
Would that I
Too, could fly
Lightly, lightly through the air.

Like a wee, crystal star
I should drift, I should blow
Near, more near,
To my dear
Where he comes through the snow.

I should fly to my love
Like a flake in the storm,
I should die,
I should die,
On his lips that are warm.

Enrichment Questions & Activities

- Find all the pairs of matching snowflakes
- Are snowflakes symmetrical?
- What will happen to the snowball by the warm fire?
- Describe a winter scene. Use all your senses.

HENRY WADSWORTH LONGFELLOW (1807-1882)

Henry Wadsworth Longfellow was an American poet who was part of the Fireside Poets. The Fireside Poets was a group of popular 19th century American poets whose works were enjoyed by ordinary people – families sitting around the fireplace in the evenings.

Enrichment Activity

Start your own fireside poetry tradition. Gather with your family and friends (a fireplace is optional) and ask each person to bring a poem to share. Make this a regular ritual in your household.

THE ARROW AND THE SONG

Henry Wadsworth Longfellow

I shot an arrow into the air,
It fell to earth, I knew not where;
For, so swiftly it flew, the sight
Could not follow it in its flight.

I breathed a song into the air,
It fell to earth, I knew not where;
For who has sight so keen and strong,
That it can follow the flight of song?

Long, long afterward, in an oak
I found the arrow, still unbroke;
And the song, from beginning to end,
I found again in the heart of a friend.

Enrichment Activity

Sing a song that is in your heart.

from THE SONG OF HIAWATHA

Henry Wadsworth Longfellow

NOTE: Hiawatha is a Native American boy who is being raised by his grandmother Nokamis. This excerpt is a part of an epic poem about his life.

When he heard the owls at midnight,
Hooting, laughing in the forest,
"What is that?" he cried in terror;
"What is that?" he said, "Nokomis?"
And the good Nokomis answered :
"That is but the owl and owlet,
Talking in their native language,
Talking, scolding at each other."

Then the little Hiawatha
Learned of every bird its language,
Learned their names and all their secrets,
How they built their nests in Summer,
Where they hid themselves in Winter,
Talked with them whene'er he met them,
Called them "Hiawatha's Chickens."

Illustrations by John James Audubon 1827-1838

Finch

Cardinal

Crane   Hummingbird   Eagle   Barn Swallow

<u>Enrichment Questions and Activities</u>

- Touch each bird as you name it

- Match each type of bird to its silhouette.

- Find each bird being described:
    - At only 3 inches long, this is the smallest bird in North America.
    - This bird lives near wetlands. It can have a wingspan of 7 feet.
    - This bird of prey (or raptor) catches small animals with its sharp talons. Its keen eyes enable it to see a rabbit two miles away.

THE CHILDREN'S HOUR

Henry Wadsworth Longfellow

Between the dark and the daylight,
When the night is beginning to lower,
Comes a pause in the day's occupations,
That is known as the Children's Hour.

I hear in the chamber above me
The patter of little feet,
The sound of a door that is opened,
And voices soft and sweet.

From my study I see in the lamplight,
Descending the broad hall stair,
Grave Alice, and laughing Allegra,
And Edith with golden hair.

A whisper, and then a silence:
Yet I know by their merry eyes
They are plotting and planning together
To take me by surprise.

A sudden rush from the stairway,
A sudden raid from the hall!
By three doors left unguarded
They enter my castle wall!

They climb up into my turret
O'er the arms and back of my chair;
If I try to escape, they surround me;
They seem to be everywhere.

They almost devour me with kisses,
Their arms about me entwine,
Till I think of the Bishop of Bingen
In his Mouse-Tower on the Rhine!

Do you think, o blue-eyed banditi,
Because you have scaled the wall,
Such an old mustache as I am
Is not a match for you all!

I have you fast in my fortress,
And will not let you depart,
But put you down into the dungeon
In the round-tower of my heart.

And there will I keep you forever,
Yes, forever and a day,
Till the walls shall crumble to ruin,
And moulder in dust away!

Enrichment Questions and Activities

- Who do *you* keep locked in the tower of your heart?

- Henry Wadsworth Longfellow wrote this poem for his three daughters. Write a poem for someone you love.

Extra Credit: MORE POEMS TO LEARN BY HEART

A century ago, every child would have been expected to memorize poetry regularly in school. Today, however, poetry memorization and recitation is a lost art form. When a child commits a poem to memory, he or she is using cognitive skills that are crucial to many other areas of learning. Reciting that poem is a wonderful exercise in public speaking.

Although all the poems in this book lend themselves to memorization, this section contains additional poems, of progressive difficulty, which are especially well suited for learning by heart. You may find that your child memorizes poems simply by hearing you read them aloud multiple times. Children as young as two years old can learn long poems in this manner. Those who prefer a more formal approach to memorization and recitation, can utilize the following tips:

- Start with the shortest poems, and take your time before moving to progressively harder ones. You'll notice that once poem memorization becomes part of your routine, your child will become faster and more efficient at learning subsequent poems by heart.

- Work on one stanza at a time. Do not move on until your child has completely mastered the stanza you are working on. This pace will vary based on the individual child.

- Read aloud each line of the stanza and ask your child to repeat after you. Then combine two lines and repeat the process until the child can repeat the entire stanza.

- If you wish, you may add hand motions or other gestures to help your child remember each part of the poem.

- Invite your child to recite the poem while standing on a stage (chair or table), in front of the mirror, or performing for an audience of family and friends.

WEATHER

Anonymous

Whether the weather be fine,
Or whether the weather be not,
Whether the weather be cold,
Or whether the weather be hot,
We'll weather the weather
Whatever the weather,
Whether we like it or not!

Enrichment Questions

- Can you figure out what each weather symbol means?
- How would you dress for each type of weather?
- Does the temperature go up or down as the weather gets warmer?
- Which type of weather is your favorite? Why?

MOSES SUPPOSES HIS TOESES ARE ROSES

Anonymous

Moses supposes his toeses are roses,
But Moses supposes erroneously,
For nobody's toeses are posies of roses,
As Moses supposes his toeses to be.

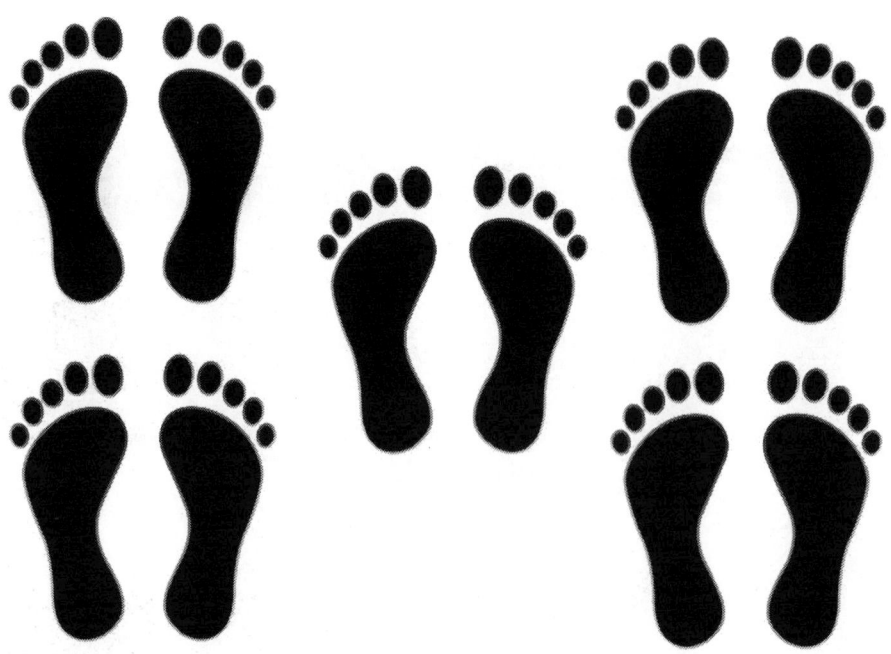

Enrichment Questions

- How many toes do you have?

- How many toes do two kids have all together? How about three kids? How many toes do the five kids in the picture have? (count by 10s)

- How many kids do you need to have 100 toes all together?

THE EARLY MORNING
Hilaire Belloc

The moon on the one hand, the dawn on the other:
The moon is my sister, the dawn is my brother.
The moon on my left and the dawn on my right.
My brother, good morning: my sister, good night.

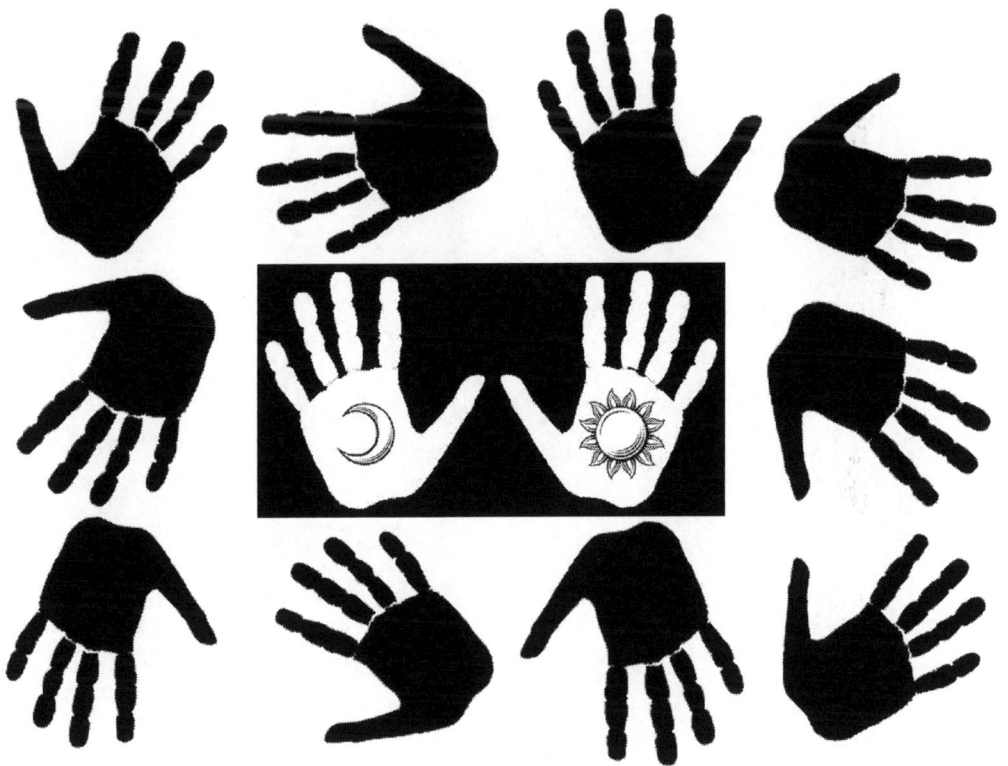

Enrichment Questions and Activities

- Which hand is your left hand? Which one is your right?
- Figure out which of the hands in the picture are right hands and which are left hands.
- Does the sun rise in the East or the West?

I'M GLAD THE SKY IS PAINTED BLUE

Anonymous

I'm glad the sky is painted blue,
And the earth is painted green,
With such a lot of nice fresh air
All sandwiched in between.

Enrichment Questions and Activity

- What tools does a painter need?

- Name an object for each color of the rainbow (red, orange, yellow, green, blue, purple).

- Paint (or draw) a landscape using as many different colors as you can.

A FARM PICTURE

Walt Whitman

Through the ample open door of the peaceful country barn,
A sun-lit pasture field, with cattle and horses feeding;
And haze, and vista, and the far horizon, fading away.

Enrichment Activity

Go outdoors and spend a couple minutes observing the landscape. When you return inside, use only your words to "paint a picture" of what you saw for someone.

THE LITTLE TURTLE
Vachel Lindsay

There was a little turtle.
He lived in a box.
He swam in a puddle.
He climbed on the rocks.

He snapped at a mosquito.
He snapped at a flea.
He snapped at a minnow.
And he snapped at me.

He caught the mosquito.
He caught the flea.
He caught the minnow.
But he didn't catch me.

Enrichment Questions

- Land turtles have legs for walking on land, while sea turtles have flippers for swimming. What kind of turtle is in the picture?

- Do turtles give birth to their young or lay eggs?

- Are turtles mammals, reptiles, or amphibians? How do you know?

THE ELF AND THE DORMOUSE

Oliver Herford

Under a toadstool crept a wee Elf,
Out of the rain to shelter himself.
Under the toadstool, sound asleep,
Sat a big Dormouse all in a heap.

Trembled the wee Elf, frightened and yet
Fearing to fly away lest he get wet.
To the next shelter—maybe a mile!
Sudden the wee Elf smiled a wee smile.

Tugged till the toadstool toppled in two.
Holding it over him, gaily he flew.
Soon he was safe home, dry as could be.
Soon woke the Dormouse—"Good gracious me!"

"Where is my toadstool?" loud he lamented.
-And that's how umbrellas first were invented.

Enrichment Activity

Pick a household object and make up a silly story about how this object was invented

from ALL ROUND THE YEAR

Edith Nesbit

What o'clock is it, children dear?
Ask of the dandelions here!
*Blow, blow, blow, and away they go—
But they do not tell us the time you know!*

Say, what month is it, children dear?
*We think it is August because we hear
The swing of the sickle, restless and slow,
And that's a sign of the month, you know.*

Enrichment Questions and Activities

- Read the time on the clocks. How could you tell the time without a clock on a sunny day?

- Put these time intervals in order: day, minute, hour, second.

- How many days are in a week? Can you name them?

- Name the months of the year. How could you tell which month it is without a calendar?

HAIKU
Matsuo Basho

Another year is gone
A traveler's shade on my head,
Straw sandals at my feet

Enrichment Questions and Activities

- How old were you on your last birthday? How old will you be on your next birthday?

- Make a list of things you want to do next year.

LEISURE

William Henry Davies

What is this life if, full of care,
We have no time to stand and stare?–

No time to stand beneath the boughs,
And stare as long as sheep and cows:

No time to see, when woods we pass,
Where squirrels hide their nuts in grass:

No time to see, in broad daylight,
Streams full of stars, like skies at night:

No time to turn at Beauty's glance,
And watch her feet, how they can dance:

No time to wait till her mouth can
Enrich that smile her eyes began?

A poor life this if, full of care,
We have no time to stand and stare.

Enrichment Question

- Which part of your body do you use to see? ..to hear? ..to smell? ..to taste? ..to touch?

- How long can you stand quietly without moving? Try making different poses like a statue.

SOMETHING TOLD THE WILD GEESE
Rachel Field

Something told the wild geese
It was time to go,
Though the fields lay golden
Something whispered, "snow."

Leaves were green and stirring,
Berries, luster-glossed,
But beneath warm feathers
Something cautioned, "frost."

All the sagging orchards
Steamed with amber spice,
But each wild breast stiffened
At remembered ice.

Something told the wild geese
It was time to fly,
Summer sun was on their wings,
Winter in their cry.

<u>Enrichment Questions and Activities</u>

- Where do geese fly in the autumn? What is this called?

- What do squirrels do to prepare for winter?

- How does a bear spend the winter?

from a LETTER TO HIS DAUGHTER
Ralph Waldo Emerson

Finish each day and be done with it.
You have done what you could.
Some blunders and absurdities
no doubt have crept in;
forget them as soon as you can.
Tomorrow is a new day;
begin it well and serenely
and with too high a spirit
to be cumbered with
your old nonsense.
This day is all that is
good and fair.
It is too dear,
with its hopes and invitations
to waste a moment on yesterdays.

Enrichment Questions and Activities

- Writing a letter is one way to send a message to someone. What are some other forms of communication?

- In this letter, Ralph Waldo Emerson gives his daughter some advice. What advice do you want to give to someone you love?

IN BEAUTY MAY I WALK

a Navajo Prayer

In beauty may I walk
All day long may I walk
Through the returning seasons may I walk
Beautifully will I possess again
Beautifully birds,
Beautifully joyful birds
On the trail marked with pollen may I walk
With grasshoppers about my feet may I walk
With dew about my feet may I walk
With beauty may I walk
With beauty before me may I walk
With beauty behind me may I walk
With beauty above me may I walk
With beauty all around me may I walk
In old age, wandering on a trail of beauty, lively, may I walk
In old age, wandering on a trail of beauty, living again, may I walk
It is finished in beauty.
It is finished in beauty.

Enrichment Question

Are the people in the picture ordered by height or age?

ABOUT THE EDITOR

Lilac Mohr is a software engineer, homeschooling parent, blogger, and entrepreneur. In 2012, she left her fourteen year career in the high tech industry to home educate her children and develop La La Logic, a critical thinking curriculum for preschoolers. Lilac enjoys combining classical education principles with modern technology to create products that can challenge children of different ages and abilities. She holds a B.S. degree in Computer Information Systems and an M.S. degree in Statistics.

Classic Poetry for Your Little Genius was inspired by Lilac's own little geniuses with whom she wanted to share her love of poetry. You can read her early education blog at http://learnersinbloom.blogspot.com.

Also available from Lilac Mohr:

La La Logic Critical Thinking Curriculum
http://www.lalalogic.com

The La La Logic Curriculum for children ages 3-6 is comprised of 100 learning units. Each unit includes an online brain challenge consisting of engaging brain training exercises disguised as computer games, a printable worksheet full of cutting and gluing, and two extension activities for parents and children to complete together.

Attribute Logic Multi-Level Learning System
https://www.thegamecrafter.com/games/attribute-logic

Attribute Logic uses hands-on manipulatives to improve your child's mathematical reasoning, visual perceptions, and critical thinking skills. The challenges include analogies, syllogisms, Raven's matrices, classification problems, and more.

Grid Logic Multi-Level Learning System
https://www.thegamecrafter.com/games/grid-logic

Grid Logic is a series of multi-level learning games and activities to improve your child's problem solving skills. These games include grid coordinate identification, an introduction to algorithm development and 4x4 Sudoku using hands-on manipulatives.

Printed in Great Britain
by Amazon